THE 80-MINUTE MINDSET

The 80-Minute Mindset

VINCE MAZZIO

The 80-Minute Mindset
Turning Practice Sessions into Execution for the
Young Athlete

Vince Mazzio

ISBN: 979-8-218-86138-4

Engagement inquiries can be requested at
80minutemindset@gmail.com

Preface

*Scholarships for softball are competitive. Only about **7.8% of high school players** continue their careers in college, with just **1.6%** making it to NCAA D1.*
Courtesy NCS College Recruiting

Who is This Book Written For?

The 80-Minute Mindset began as a quick sound bite describing a specific way to approach coaching young athletes. This book was originally meant to be a summary of that method and used as a guide for softball coaches taking on a new role, a new team, a new age group.

But, as it evolved, and feedback came in from all sorts of respected coaches, teachers and mentors from a variety of ages, it became more universal. It became apparent that many folks who coach and mentor are facing the challenge of providing meaningful practice sessions that result in higher level performance sessions. And so now, this book is meant to inspire reflection about the connection between differences players feel as they grow, how they approach preparation, and the way they perform at different points in their life with respect to the sports, and other endeavors they participate in.

> **Dear Coaches,**
>
> *Yes, you played college baseball...competitive softball is a different game. You played college softball...the player today is not the player from yester year. Your experience is not their experience. Make every effort to understand their world now – not your world in the 80's or 90's, 2000's. Don't worry, the singer of Glory Days will understand.*

Yes, the content may focus on the 80-minute timed game of travel softball, but the concepts are transferable to all formats and all ages. *Every time you see the word "softball" please insert their sport, their team, their experience.*

So then,

HOW do they love the game?
(very important you know the answer)

One of the biggest challenges to coaching is getting a team moving in one direction, while still maintaining the relevant and purposeful support for each individual player. Using every tool in the toolbox is necessary to build that connection. The question "Do they love the game?" is semi-basic. We can safely assume they have more than "a like" for the game if they are spending so much time on it. *What we really need to know is "how" do they love it?* Know that some may aspire to a college experience and some may want very competitive softball *until* college. Or there could be many reasons in between. To get everyone moving together, while still coaching individuals, you need to know the difference.

Do you?

Introduction

What in the world is this!? Many years ago, watching my first travel softball game (after years of Little League/Rec), I found I was watching a different sport. Never mind the crazy wristband plays opposing coaches were calling, or the amped-up cheers – I was confused about the structure of the game itself. *This game lasts 80 minutes? Huh?* Best case scenario that's a 5-inning game. Worst case means 3 field innings and an at-bat for each player.

Was my daughter mentally prepared for this?
But, more evident, was the TEAM ready for this?

What I quickly learned was that, yes, 80 minutes was the defined rule, but competitive softball is a unique game in and of itself. *It is a speed game!* Shorter base paths, shorter fences thus smaller gaps and yes, competitive athletes!

Fast forward a couple of years..."Don't be Mr. Coach Obvious!" *(thank you, internet sensation Domingo Ayala).* Those were my daughter's words when I said, "I am going to coach your team, are you good with that?" She followed up by saying *"don't tell me I need to do something, show me how to do it, show me how to play this game...show US how it works! Oh...and be consistent!"*

That got me to thinking...can a coach who grew up playing baseball teach the fundamentals of skill building, and efficiency, and speed, all while managing the ups and downs of essentially a different sport? A sport in which some coaches usually just say minutes before an 8 am game, "let's get fired up, let's get started quick, let's go!" The answer is a resounding **not in the traditional sense!**

It takes coaching a *mindset*. A mindset that preaches understanding how the performance task is supposed to go and then building a routine of "real-life" foundational practice. A mindset that a game in this version does not always last for 7 innings. It takes minute-by-minute efficiency, requires a different personal growth trajectory, and is won at the margins. It takes melding this mindset with the developing player. ***There is an opportunity to not just coach a team but support the skill of approaching new experiences.***

For an adolescent/teen managing change already, training needs to occur well before 7:55 am Game Day. In no way do these players have an on/off switch. *Training must follow suit! Training that supports a heightened focus for a defined period of time, and increases the likelihood of successful execution of learned and practiced skills.*

Initial Reaction

"So, you're just going to do this mind stuff...no drills, no fielding, no hitting?" That was a parent question early on. I politely responded that I would still be drilling on throwing, fielding, baserunning and hitting. We will still focus on developing skills. It will just be more purposeful, intentional, promote growth, and make executing in game situations an easier process for each player.

Two days later the same parent said, "it was 15 minutes before my daughter picked up a ball this practice." I said "that is correct."

Eight months later the same parent said "my daughter has never been more positive about playing softball."

Chapter 1

The Why

Tuesday...great practice. Thursday...great practice. Saturday game...?

We have all been there. The team gets to the game and the same mistakes addressed in practice seem to find their way into every aspect of the game. In moments of frustration, we say crazy stuff to ourselves like *"they were at practice, right"* and *"we did go through this, right Bob?"* And the more frustrated we get, the more we either question the players' desire (they must want it more than me!) or their motivations. Hopefully, we soon realize they are still not only developing players but also developing humans. Maybe they aren't even sure *why* they are playing a competitive sport. And then, *how* do they love it? (remember that maybe sorta' college thing?)

I'm a former Social Studies teacher, so let me drop some history on you. On a trip to historic Valley Forge National Park, my family and I read a display describing the training of the American Army there - led by Baron von Steuben. Because things were looking bleak, and we were getting our butts kicked a bit, von Steuben had to adjust his teaching (coaching). Here is his quote from that display:

> *"The genius of this nation is not in the least to be compared with the Prussians, the Austrians or French. (there) you say to your soldier 'do this' and he does it. But I am obliged to say to the American, 'This is the reason why you ought to do that and then he does it."*

von Steuben worked tirelessly on teaching (coaching) marching and maneuvering techniques in different ways at Valley Forge, and when it came time for battle, well...you know the rest.

Pause and let this fact sink in...some dude in 1778 realized that people learn and perform better when they realize their "why." And further, when they realize that "battling" over and over again loses out every time to *thoughtful* and *purposeful* preparation, great progress occurs. As you read on through this book, think back to those reflections.

My dad used to say when I was young that, for a job to be meaningful, I had to be able to laugh while doing it. I now think I understood what he was saying. He thought that a job should be so aligned to what fulfilled you that you could smile regularly while doing it.

Today, Simon Sinek is largely credited with the phrase "Start with Why." Sinek (2009) has created a whole movement around the phrase. (Maybe Dad was ahead of his time!) Sinek has said that, when we work hard on something we don't care about, it causes stress. But, when we love the work, it brings fulfillment. There is no reason we can't begin introducing this idea at a younger age. In fact, as coaches, teachers and mentors, we owe that to our players. Then, Sinek believes that once kids understand their *why*, they can figure out *how* to get there. This is where you can offer great support. How can you help?

Players in early development (and beyond) regularly experience genuine barriers to translating a great week of practice to successful game performance. Perhaps your help can start with addressing these barriers. These can include the following, which will be alluded to in later chapters:

- Performance Anxiety and Pressure
- Lack of Transferable Practice
- Overthinking Movements
- Peer and Social Pressure

For the record, here is **My Why**...as in why I believe in *The 80-Minute Mindset* as a coaching framework. It all lies in my response to the parent mentioned earlier.

We will drill as individual players and as a team. But we will do it with purpose - breaking skills down to basic building blocks - at the same time addressing player responses to possible barriers.

All with the goal of getting to game day prepared to seamlessly execute and succeed – no matter the situation.

I want to support game day execution.
I want to support building transferable skills for a lifetime of success in sports and beyond.

Chapter 2

The Philosophy

In **General,** The 80-Minute Mindset requires training that promotes these ideas:

1. **The Play is Never Over...no heads ever looking at the ground.** With 80 minutes there is literally no time to do dwell on a mistake – as the play will continue and the next play is coming soon. We all strive for this in our professional lives so we should train our players for this. *As a coach, mimic this as much as possible!* I have always held 80 minutes of practice in each session. Any gaps in between tournament games ONLY included chunks of 80 minutes of downtime. Etc, etc. you get the idea.

2. **Muscle Memory**...Skill development and preparation that results in minimal time spent on in-game decision making...no matter what variables occur!

3. **Efficiency**...80 minutes only allows for certain behaviors and actions. Other actions need to be left behind and cannot be allowed on the field. Self-pity and sulking are time wasters (see "I Got You).

Specifically then, what is the 80-Minute Mindset?

These CORE VALUES

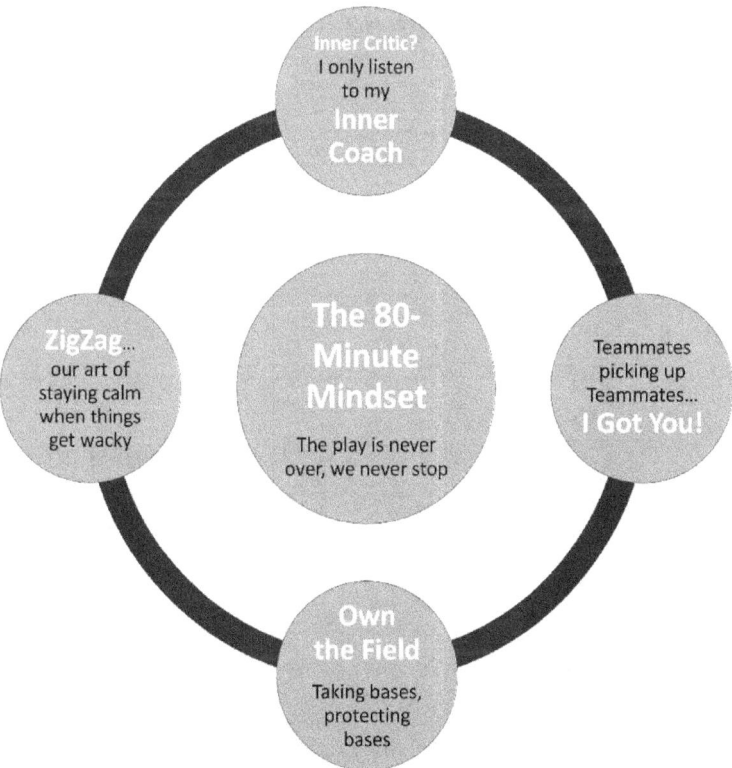

The following chapters will break these core values down in practical ways supported by science and research.

But first a note on communication...

All these ideas and routines need to be captured, communicated and drilled to support performance execution – in a way that is pleasing to, and accepted by the crowd (the team). I call it...

Sound Bites!

Understanding the attention span of the developing teen is critical to the structure of practice and performance. Unfortunately, today, our teens have been exposed to gathering their info from social media. Some researched facts:

- Social media "hits" (reels) occur in 30 second to 2-minute bursts.
- The average session-length attention span for an 11-16 year-old ranges from 25-40 minutes.
- The average statement attention is *8.25 seconds!*

Great facts! What do they mean?! Well:

- Social media has retrained our brains. We must acknowledge and adapt.

· In an 80-minute practice, don't waste 4 minutes talking - players should be building *their own* capacity (more to come).

Speak in **Sound Bites!**

Sound Bite: n. a short memorable phrase that captures a message and is easily remembered and repeatable.

Chapter 3

Building the Inner Coach

Inner Critic?
I only listen to my
Inner Coach

We all get into coaching with the noble aspiration to affect change, to teach, to make a difference. Many times, we feel that what we *bring* is what they *need*. But hopefully we soon realize that reaching 11 players on an 11-player team is a challenge. Every player has unique needs for growth, communicates differently, responds to coaching differently, and the list goes on. Soon, the one-size-fits-all approach seems as tiny as a golf ball in an ocean. This realization is okay but, man, humility is hard! John Wooden, legendary basketball coach for UCLA once said that *"...a coach's humility is revealed in the way he lis-*

tens, adapts, and believes in each player's unique strength - not just the obvious ones. That's where transformation begins."

The goal then, is to re-focus and determine "how do I give each player what they need, on a regular basis, to grow their skills?" A solid possible answer is to increase capacity. The **best** answer is to increase **their** capacity!

Their capacity. The adolescent/teen brain is an interesting one. The tangles are frequent. Layer in the hormonal changes, and the challenge to coach increases. As a coach, it is essential to learn to change the speaker inside your player's heads - and increase THEIR capacity to coach.

Too often, the default for a teenager is "why I am wrong." The (performance) anxiety centers around judgment - from themselves and their peers. *Building the inner coach means changing that default to "how can I be right."* The end goal is to get them to reflect on how they can improve, to build their self-coaching capacity and their game IQ.

Here are some examples:

Player Action	Inner Critic says...	Inner Coach might say...
Watched 3rd Strike	I always wait too long!	While on the bench, I am going to watch this ump to learn his/her strike zone.
Swing and Miss	I can't hit the high pitch!	Letters-high is not my power zone. What is MY power zone? Know that next at bat.
Error	I stink on balls to my left	Know the hitters. Maybe I need to shift. Then, next week at practice I will focus on moving to my left.

There's Gotta' Be Some Science!

Adolescents and teens can't easily see where they are, versus where they can be. Help them! Mr. Coach Obvious would merely tell the player, "visualize success." For most players, they can't. Visualizing success **is** the issue!

Carol Dweck is widely considered the originator of the *Growth Mindset.* This is the idea that abilities can be developed through effort and learning. This is opposed to the *fixed mindset* which says our abilities are static.

What? **Growth Mindset?** It's just school talk. You know, the latest and greatest.

When I read *The Performance Paradox* (2023) by Eduardo Briceno, a colleague of Dweck, I laughed. He provided an example of growth mindset that I insist was based on me (it *wasn't*, but it was very relevant!). Here is my experience with **his** typing example...You would think that all of us who type everyday would be classified as world-class typists, right? I know I send some high-quality emails every day that require lots of typing. I type with 4 fingers. Every day, over and over...I type...and I am an average typist at best. Perhaps I should spend some time on tried-and-true typing technique before performing some email magic?...yes!

Briceno also cites the fact the movie "King Richard" revealed that Venus and Serena Williams spent YEARS practicing before playing a tournament. The result? They entered their first game trusting their instincts. We can probably agree they have done well.

WHY? And what does that have to do with coaching an 80-minute game?

Performance Zone vs. Learning Zone (Briceno, 2023)

- **Performance Zone** = Outcomes. In this zone, a Coach is ONLY concerned with outcomes.

- ○ If you only ask players to live in the performance zone, they will not improve. I always chuckle when a parent says, "we have to hustle out after the game, my daughter is guest playing for another team, you know...her other team is pretty good."
- The **Learning Zone** involves breaking down the areas needed for improvement to small chunks. It **IS** a purposeful, targeted area of practice which requires reflection and understanding. It **IS NOT** an adult giving 2,3,4 directions on every pitch, repetition.

Briceno (2023) gives another great example talking about reflection in the Learning Zone. He tells the story of violinist Nathan Milstein. Milstein realized he practiced much less than others. When asked why he made such gains while others did not, he said, *"it doesn't really matter how long, but, if you practice with your fingers, no amount is enough, if you practice with your head two hours is plenty"*

Now to connect to the why. Dweck tested, researched and published multiple points of research demonstrating that constant praise conditions for people to do things for approval, rather than help them develop their *intrinsic interests and motivations.*

Dweck (2006) defines internal motivation as; *"helping us become deeper learners, gives us more agency over our actions and fosters the resilience needed in the face of adversity."* This growth mindset approach leads players to believe that success can be the result of *purposeful* hard work. This growth mindset approach supports the translation of practice to game day performance.

So, the "why" becomes increased performance in games, increased competitive satisfaction, or increased chances at achieving longer term goals. You, as coach, should know what your players want to achieve. *(see page 5, wink wink).*

> **Coaches Tip**
> *Try not to praise EVERYTHING!* It's hard. But when a player mistake happens, try not to only say "it's okay." Say, where do you think you go from here?

The 80-Minute Response

Do not allow slumping shoulders. That is an inner-critic behavior. Stop your players when they do that. Encourage and teach them to self-correct by asking "who are you listening to, your **inner critic**, or **inner coach**?"

The inner critic is overwhelming and brings them down. The inner coach trains them to see failure as temporary and forces them to make a plan for improvement next time.

As a coach, channel your inner John Wooden and model that for them. Say things like, "wow, my play there didn't work, let me rethink that!" When they commit an error, strike out, etc., let them emote for a moment, then, **insist** they answer the question of who they are listening to.

Chapter 4

I Got You

Teammates
picking up
Teammates
I Got You!

This value begins a journey in failure and ends triumphantly in resilience. How do humans react to failure? If not managed properly, it can weigh us down. For teen players searching for identity, it is the weight of the world. In a game with time, or innings-limits, this can have significant impact. *Think of the math,* if a player is mentally bogged down by 1 play for 10 minutes, that is $1/8^{th}$ of an 80-minute game. Or, if it lasts 1 inning of a 7-inning game, it is just too long!

On the field, we have all been witness to the after-effect of an error or a strikeout. Sometimes, for a player:

It. Lasts. A. Long. Time.

The easy line a coach will say is "we need you on the *next* play." True, that is a fact. But does it provide foundational support?

My dad would say "send it out with the trash." He was right. Today, though, it is harder. It is not a one and done. That is because, at any given moment, none of us know who the player is more influenced by – the coach, the parent, or their peers. My guess it would mostly be their peers (thank you history, and social media).

So, maybe, just maybe, the challenge for coaches is to shift the lense of approval from coach to peer.

There's Gotta' Be Some Science!

Smith and McDonough (2009) in *The Journal of Sport Behavior* described the peer affect as "a sensitivity to judgment which heightens self-consciousness and detracts from focus during competition."

Beilock and Carr (2001) in *The Journal of Experimental Psychology* attributed performance anxiety and pressure to an actual cognitive interference. They found that anxiety "disrupts focus and motor coordination, leading to impaired performance."

Do you hear that?! Some really smart people have re-affirmed what we all know - when we are nervous about how we will be perceived, how people will judge us, we just don't perform as well. In my professional life, at my age, that is a consideration. Think of what that means for the developing teen. Aye, aye! The peer effect is real!

As adults, we have learned the tricks to minimize this. Or, our maturity and experience has steeled us to face this. Now, we must help our players to build these skills.

The 80-Minute Response

Now that we've established root causes, as coaches we must ask some questions. To quote soccer legend Mia Hamm, *"Failure happens all the time. It happens every day in practice. What makes you better is how you react to it."* As coaches, how do we teach and build resilience? How do we show the player that mistakes will happen, and the game is not over?

We MUST start with the building blocks:

1. As coach, **build confidence in the face of risk.** That is, when a player approaches a performance situation where failure is a possibility, they should feel quipped to execute. For example, I always want to be the most aggressive team on the basepaths. In order to do that, I encourage the players to always look to take the next base. I had to make that risk safe. So, I would say, if you get caught stealing *it's on me.* And I would say that loudly - so the whole team and crowd could hear - if they ever got caught.

2. **Build self-awareness.** Don't tell them what they did wrong, *ask them* if they know how they

could have "done that differently. Or "what is your inner coach saying?"

3. ***Build a mindset for growth.*** Every game, every practice is an opportunity to improve.
4. ***Stress player resilience.*** Not everything will go your way!
5. ***Encourage players to take charge.*** You have learned what their motivation is - their "why". Demonstrate that if this is what you truly want, you have to want to improve...for yourself. Make independent decisions to do so.

These are all good foundational building blocks and yes, the thought of failure needs to disappear, but it does not just happen when you say to players "take care of each other!"

MOST IMPORTANTLY - recognize whose opinion matters. Later, in the "Build the Drill" Section, you will see an example of how peer support can be tangible. In general though, take every opportunity to encourage teammates to verbalize, clearly and loudly, support for their peers.

As for coaches, I would suggest...a **Sound Bite!** A sound bite that takes the idea of peer judgment and turns it into actionable peer support and affirmation.

I Got You!

Chapter 5

ZigZag

ZigZag

our art of staying calm when things get wacky

Parent 1: *throw it home !!!!!!*

Parent 2: *throw it to 3rd !!!!!!*

Shortstop: hit the cut (she's right)

Brain: What should I do????

The multiple exclamations are not grammatical errors. They are meant to portray in-game chaos. We've all been there. The world of perceived, or real chaos.

It is exactly how many coach text threads, or post tournament beers, or spousal conversation downloads go, where we have all said, "it just seems that we play good all game except for THAT ONE INNING!" Yes, that one inning. The one where the ball gets thrown around, the other bench is loud, opposing parents are obnoxious, and we start with 1 mistake and soon the snowball is an avalanche.

In addition to meeting the challenge of that one inning, ZigZag is also the foundational step to finishing games. Back to the postgame analysis - "we just need to figure out how to finish." That is true, but it does take practice. Managing the stress of "that inning" is a thing. A thing that needs to be rehearsed.

What do we do? We **ZigZag!** We become more focused when things get wacky! Does that happen by saying "deep breath everyone!" Absolutely not!

There's Gotta' Be Some Science!

Phil Jackson (2013) says *"I've always been interested in getting players to think for themselves so that they can make difficult decisions in the heat of battle."* I trust Phil. He won a lot of games. But he also has a reputation for focusing on the mental aspect of sport.

In *The Journal of Experimental Psychology* (1979), Shea and Morgan spoke about how context affects the acquisition, retention, and transfer of motor skill. (Don't worry, I had to re-read that myself to put it in plain language). Essentially, in **no way** does the traditional "Situations" drill in practice provide anything close to the context of a game. The summary for Shea and Morgan's research on this is:

> Blocked Practice (predictable environments) = **BAD**
>
> Random practice (mimicking game scenarios) = **GOOD**

So, coaches must seek ways to provide the "real life" aspect to practice. Researchers Robert and Elizabeth Bjork (2011) call this the idea of "desirable difficulties." What they mean is that practices should have the right amount of difficulty to promote growth. *It does not mean harder is better.* It means we should seek to find an element of difficulty for each drill to build the skill while mirroring the right level of chaos and pressure a player or team will encounter in a game.

The 80-Minute Response

Treavor Reagan of *The Learning Lab* says to get the players out of their comfort zone. He believes players need to learn skills in the context they will use them. The "context" is the game. Reagan describes the game as one of uncertainty, unpredictability and pressure.

So, *build these characteristics into your practices.* Over time, they focus no matter what is thrown at them.

I am a proud St. Joe Hawk alum. I love seeing my Facebook feed from SJU filled with basketball players practicing and training. Weird, I know. In one scene, there will be a player looking to make a layup with 2 coaches waving giant pads in their face or banging them on their shoulders. The focus the players have under that practice condition is amazing. *When those players enter a game, they know the feeling!*

The Philadelphia 76ers have a great, and fairly new tradition of having sponsors provide free items to fans when opposing teams miss 2 foul shots in a row. The fans are out-of-control loud during that free throw. Brikin' for _____ (omitted for copyright purposes, but you get the idea) has become huge at their arena. Imagine being a visiting player standing at the line, hearing some chant that has nothing to do with basketball while trying to perform a very basic skill!?

You are saying, "Vince, for real?" I am responding "yes, for real."

When we build focus in the face of chaos, we build not only high performers in softball, but also character for the future.

To know me is to know I like a bit of fun. During the Taylor Swift Eras tour, I had a big opportunity. I would regularly get everyone started on a fast-paced drill that had performance goals (ex. 10 rotations without error) and, just as they were humming, I would break out the blue-tooth speaker of Taylor favorites and sing and dance crazy. If they didn't make the play, we would do it again. Or, during fielding drills, I would suddenly take tennis balls and throw them at the fielder.

Very important reflective close on this chapter: Bring the players in at the end of these drills and ask "why do you think I did that?" Don't rush through these post drill talks.

They are crucial to the retention and transfer of practice to game.

Coaches Tip

Be bold! Don't be afraid to be creative in creating chaos in practice. The players will laugh at first and say, "is this guy/gal serious?" but over time they will say "you can't distract me!"

Chapter 6

Own the Field

> **Own the Field**
> Taking bases,
> Protecting bases

For those of you who have been saying, "but what about the softball?"

As a Philadelphian, it pains me to say this. Chip Kelly, now coach of wherever, says this: *everybody has the same amount of time during the day...you can either just spend it or, you can invest it (in yourself)."*

So why not invest in yourself and own the field? In this case, owning the field is a mindset that is built by quantities of *purposeful practice* reps. When you provide players an opportunity to engage in purposeful reps, they are investing in themselves. Reps that translate to game day execution - they are doing it for themselves.

Remember, adolescents and teens have no on/off switch. Whatever they rehearse repeatedly in practice will be the norm in games. Recently, I chuckled at a coach who said "we ask and coach the girls to be more aggressive during league/tournament games than we do for scrimmages." **Head scratcher alert!** Being aggressive is a learned behavior. Learning to take an extra base, make an aggressive throw, etc. is a learned, muscle memory behavior.

To establish guidelines on time and place for core behavior severely dampens muscle memory and confidence.

There's Gotta' Be Some Science!

Practice is the time for mechanics. Practice is the time to create automaticity, otherwise known as muscle memory. Beilock, et.al., in a 2002 bulletin focuses on a hypothesis that says when teens are constantly monitoring their mechanics during games, muscle memory - *automaticity is actually disrupted*!

I'll leave that science right there.

The 80-Minute Response

As a coach, we have all experienced the in-game hitting instruction urge. If we are talking about building the inner coach, such as encouraging the player to examine the ump's strike zone - then...**yes!** But ask yourself, does a parent yelling from the sideline on every pitch promote automaticity, or reduce overthinking, or alleviate perfor-mance anxiety, or increase focus, or, I could go on for another 173 words. In short, make mental notes for ad-dressing mechanics for practice. Then, create a drill which recalls that behavior, corrects it, and recreates a game condition to rehearse it.

On a more team or global scale, owning a softball field starts with acknowledging the fact that there is both of-fense and defense. *Thanks Mr. Coach Obvious!* For each offensive skill we strive to master, there is a mirrored de-fensive skill. Break your concepts down to foundational Offensive and Defensive roots, and then teach them to-gether to build the "owning" mentality.

*"Coach, you said in September that these are **MY** bases, I believed you."*

For the below examples, try teaching them in tandem. Start by teaching and drilling the offensive side, then switch to the same scenario on the defensive side.

Scenario	Offense	Defense
Bunting	<ul><li>Teach correct form</li><li>Model it</li><li>Have all drill</li></ul>	<ul><li>Explain rotations</li><li>Create all contingencies</li><li>Have all drill in all potential positions</li></ul>
Aggressive baserunning	<ul><li>Teach the scenarios</li><li>Teach the "cues"</li><li>Opposition not paying attention,</li><li>Catcher throwing high, pitcher not in circle, etc.</li><li>Set them free</li></ul>	<ul><li>Revisit the scenarios</li><li>Drill the cues - that is, crisp return throws, heads never down, expect the other team to run, etc.</li></ul>

Chapter 7

Build the Drill

If, at any time in this book you said, "yeah, yeah, yeah, nice thought but give me a drill" and jumped to this chapter, I implore you to go back and finish the chapter and read the whole book. The context is important for these drills, or the many others you create or adapt to achieve their purpose.

This book is meant to be a framework for coaching a philosophy or system. The following drills are either original, or have "80-Minute Mindset" adaptations, or "wrinkles." In no way did I intend to provide a comprehensive catalog of drills - the global intraweb can provide that for you. The few examples show how every single drill can encompass adaptations that incorporate the Mindset - thereby increasing the likelihood of gameday execution of skills and plays practiced during the week.

But First, The Method
We all have our favorite drills. We know them, the players know them. But, do they always get 100% ex-

ecution in games. Well, maybe not 100%, but is there room for growth towards perfection? Try this method to get closer to that number by creating game-like environments.

Start with your drill:

1. Analyze how it can be adapted to create a game context
2. Identify a Core Value
3. Give it a Sound Bite name
4. Re-Teach the drill by explaining the Why! Explain the significance of the Sound Bite – that you will repeat this word, phrase, constantly so that the players know what it means, even in the midst of the game.
5. Stay true to it. Demonstrate it is something they can count on.

Now, the examples

Core Value: The Inner Coach

Sound Bite: 1 Pitch Mentality
Original Drill: Live Pitching Batting Practice
Objective: To make BP mirror a real game context in which hitters quickly decide on each pitch depending on the count and the situation:

Why: BP is about reps, reps, reps and, while there is a place for that, this different format allows players to focus on what they know about the ump's strike zone *(the only one that matters)*, the pitcher and what they can do to make the most of 1 pitch.

How: Split the team in groups that make sense perhaps evenly, or maybe just have 3 batters at a time. In rapid succession, have each batter line up for 1 pitch. After the pitch, keep the count and have them return to the line. A hit gets a fresh count. As the coach, keep repeating the Sound Bite "1 Pitch Mentality." Reiterating this means there are no slumping shoulders for a strike, etc. - only 1 pitch matters! Repeat, repeat, repeat!

Core Value: I Got You

Sound Bite Activity: I Got You
Original Drill: n/a
Objective: To create a structure that fosters immediate peer support.

Why: Remember – the anxiety of performance is real! Take the judgment out of the game by getting players actively supporting each other. Also, 10 minutes of self-pity is a timewaster!

How: Every time a player makes a mistake in the field, at the plate, on the basepaths, insist that other players say "I Got You (name)". *Once the player hears that, insist she pounds her fist into her glove twice and moves on.*

Core Value: ZigZag

Sound Bite Activity: ZigZag

Original Drill: Coordinated 2 line throwing drill

Objective: To practice throwing technique and ball exchange under chaotic, game-like conditions.

Why: Throwing drills can get repetitive and yet, throws are a glaring example of how game chaos can dramatically impact performance.

How: Split the team into 2 lines. Start 1 ball at one end, and another at the opposite end/opposite side. Players will throw across the divide, skipping a player until each ball reaches the opposite end. Then, return the ball in the opposite direction. So, a player's team is every other player on each side. Both balls are thrown at once. Yes, crossing over. Do this in a race style. All the while, create as many distractions as possible – loud yelling, parents screaming, etc. Keep repeating until focus is laser-like – even under crazy conditions.

Core Value: Own The Field

Sound Bite Activity: Yellow Ball White Ball

Original Drill: Base running sprints

Objective: To train the player that the play is never over, eyes should always be on the ball, always ready to take the next base.

Why: There are so many things that must go right on the defensive side to prevent base advance. Players must never put their heads down while running. They must always see the ball. Coaches should never have players facing them (and away from the field) while coaching bases.

How: Line the players up at home. Coach stands at the pitcher's mound with 1 yellow ball and 1 white ball behind their back. Coach says "go." Player sprints to first, runs through, turns back and looks at the coach. Coach has revealed either the white or yellow ball. The player screams out the color. Do this a few reps. On the next turn, the player stays at first on white, sprints to second on yellow. Continue to add different scenarios and different bases, all the while maintaining player focus on the ball.

Chapter 8

Bring on the Closer

"There is no such thing as a new idea. It is impossible. We simply take a lot of old ideas and put them into a sort of mental kaleidoscope. We give them a turn and they make new and curious combinations."
Mark Twain

That is the crux of the 80-Minute Mindset - not creating new ideas, but creating new arrangements, new interpretations and new techniques for a new generation. It is critical for new and seasoned coaches to understand that players and their motivations change frequently. These changes require a new lense, an expanded toolbox and a comfort level with change.

As I previewed, this started out as a softball-focused, age-specific coaches manual. But, it has evolved as feedback came in. It is now a framework for all ages, all sports.

So, what to do?

· Realize Reality! Your impact is not just about this season. It has long term and lasting effects. Your method, your language and your understanding of your role and impact is real.
· Realize softball, or any other sport can be a vehicle for many life experiences.
· Get out of your comfort zone! – Spend the time to think about everything you grew up with – in rec, high school, college and decide if that is even relevant to your current players in this current time. Make a list – check it off!
· Read! – Research and understand the current landscape of players and PEOPLE. It has changed and continues to change every year.
· Meet players where they are at. Meet players where they are at (not a typo).
· Use your experience. As coaches and adults, you have great experience in what your players will be in their futures – prepare them?

Your experience is not their experience. Make every effort to understand their world now – not your world in the 80's or 90's, 2000's.

HOW do they love the game?

Smart People

Beilock, S. L., & Carr, T. H. (2001). On the fragility of skilled performance: What governs choking under pressure? Journal of Experimental Psychology: General, 130(4), 701–725.

Beilock, S. L., Carr, T. H., MacMahon, C., & Starkes, J. L. (2002). When paying attention becomes counterproductive: Impact of divided versus skill-focused attention on novice and experienced performance of sensorimotor skills. Journal of Experimental Psychology: Applied, 8(1), 6–16.

Bjork, E. L., & Bjork, R. A. (2011). Making things hard on yourself, but in a good way: Creating desirable difficulties to enhance learning. *Psychology and the real world: Essays illustrating fundamental contributions to society*, 56-64.

Briceño, E. (2023). *The performance paradox: Turning the power of mindset into action. Ballantine Books.*

Dorsch, T. E., Smith, A. L., & McDonough, M. H. (2009). Parents' perceptions of child-to-parent socialization in organized youth sport. Journal of Sport & Exercise Psychology, 31(4), 444–468.

Dweck, C. S. (2006). *Mindset: The new psychology of success.* Random House.

Jackson, P., & Delehanty, H. (2013). Eleven Rings: The Soul of Success. Penguin Press.

Reagan,Treavor: Educator and speaker known for founding "Train Ugly." (2023)

Shea, J. B., & Morgan, R. L. (1979). Contextual interference effects on the acquisition, retention, and transfer of a motor skill. Journal of Experimental Psychology: Human Learning and Memory, 5(2), 179–187. Robert and Elizabeth Bjork call this the idea of "desirable difficulties"

Sinek, S. (2009). *Start with why: how great leaders inspire everyone to take action.* Penguin.

Thank You!

To Candace, who for over 20 years has been patient and supportive and said, "yes, you should write a book."

To Taryn, who had to endure the philosophy and the aftermath.

To Dillon and Alina, who sacrificed their dad spending time with other kids.

To my bro Vic, who taught me patience, maturity, book publishing (and some coaching technique).

To those who had input into this book – the list is long.